AF506632

THE SHADOW SELF GUIDEBOOK

A Journey Into Wholeness

by

Zara Nolan

Copyright © 2024 by Zara Nolan
All rights reserved.

No portion of this book may be reproduced without written permission from the publisher or author except as permitted by U.S. copyright law, which includes fair use for educational or review purposes.
This publication is designed to provide accurate and authoritative information regarding the subject matter. However, it sold with the understanding that neither the author nor the publisher is engaged in rendering legal, investment, accounting, or other professional services. The publisher and author have used their best efforts in preparing this book but make no representations or warranties concerning the accuracy or completeness of the contents. They expressly disclaim any implied warranties of merchantability or fitness for a particular purpose. The advice and strategies included here may not be suitable for your situation, but you should be able to consult with a professional when you need them. Neither the publisher nor the author shall be liable for any loss of profit or other commercial damages, including but not limited to special, incidental, consequential, personal, or other damages.

TABLE OF CONTENTS

INTRODUCTION

UNVEILING THE PATH WITHIN

In the quiet recesses of our being lies a realm unexplored—a landscape of shadows and light waiting to be discovered. The journey inward, into the depths of our consciousness, is an adventure that unveils the intricate layers of our true selves. Within this space, we encounter our shadows—the aspects of ourselves often hidden from the world and, at times, even from our awareness.

" Shadow Self Guidebook" invites you on a transformative odyssey—a journey beyond the surface into self-discovery, exploration, and acceptance. This book is not just about acknowledging the shadows that lurk within; it is a guide that encourages embracing these shadows as integral parts of our existence, fostering a deeper understanding of the self.

In these pages, you will find pathways to navigate the complexities of your inner landscape, confront the shadows that have dwelled in the corners of your consciousness, and discover the profound wisdom that arises from acknowledging and integrating these aspects of yourself. It is an invitation to embark on a quest towards self-acceptance, compassion, and holistic growth.

This journey isn't about finding a flaw to fix or erasing parts deemed undesirable; instead, it's an embrace—an act of reclaiming all facets of ourselves, understanding that immense opportunities for growth and transformation are within the shadows.

Through reflective practices, insightful narratives, and actionable guidance, this book aims to empower you to navigate the depths of your being, cultivating resilience, authenticity, and a profound sense of inner peace.

Join me as we embark on this expedition inward, where shadows dissipate in the light of self-awareness and where embracing your depths catalyzes an extraordinary voyage of self-discovery and empowerment.

The journey begins within.

Part I:

SETTING THE FOUNDATION

"Your vision will become clear
only when you can look into
your own heart. Who looks
outside, dreams; who looks
inside, awakes."

Carl Jung

Chapter 1

UNDERSTANDING SELF-EXPLORATION

In the tapestry of human existence, each contains a vast and intricate landscape that often remains uncharted and unseen. This inner terrain houses our conscious thoughts and beliefs and the hidden recesses of our psyche—the shadows that shape our perceptions, actions, and interactions with the world.

Self-exploration, the journey inward, is an endeavor of immense significance. It is a deliberate and courageous act of turning our attention from the external clamor to the rich and nuanced world within. At its core, self-exploration is an invitation—a call to delve beneath the surface layers of our identities, beliefs, and experiences in pursuit of deeper understanding and self-awareness.

This chapter serves as a compass, guiding you through the initial steps of your inner journey. It begins with acknowledging self-exploration is not merely a one-time endeavor but an ongoing process—a continuous dialogue with ourselves that unfolds over time. It's about creating a sacred space for introspection, a sanctuary where we can observe our thoughts, emotions, and patterns without judgment.

To embark on this expedition, it's crucial to cultivate a mindset of curiosity and openness. Allow yourself to be a gentle observer of your inner landscape, embracing the light and the shadows within. Understand that these shadows, often dismissed or feared, hold profound insights and lessons waiting to be unearthed.

Moreover, self-exploration necessitates an acceptance of imperfection—a recognition that our journey within may not always be smooth or linear. There might be discomfort when confronting aspects of ourselves that challenge our perceptions. Yet, it's within these moments that growth and transformation find their fertile ground.

As you traverse this terrain of self-exploration, consider the power of inquiry. Ask yourself probing questions, allowing them to act as lanterns illuminating the obscured corners of your consciousness. Questions such as, "What beliefs shape my actions?" or "How do I respond to challenging emotions?" can catalyze deeper introspection.

Remember, self-exploration is not about seeking perfection or achieving a fixed state of being. Instead, it's a courageous endeavor—embracing the multifaceted self and accepting the complexities that make us beautifully human.

This chapter sets the stage for your expedition, laying the groundwork for a transformative journey toward self-discovery and inner harmony.

EXERCISE 1:

EXPLORING YOUR INNER LANDSCAPE

Objective: This exercise aims to initiate your journey of self-discovery by encouraging reflection on your inner landscape, thoughts, and emotions.

Instructions:

1. Quiet Space Preparation: Find a quiet and comfortable space to relax without interruptions. Sit or lie in a relaxed position, making you feel at ease.

2. Mindful Breathing: Begin by focusing on your breath. Take a few deep breaths, inhaling through your nose and exhaling through your mouth. Notice the sensation of the breath entering and leaving your body.

3. Inner Exploration Visualization:
   - Close your eyes and visualize a serene, calming, safe landscape. It could be a lush forest, a tranquil beach, or any space where you feel connected to yourself.
   - As you immerse yourself in this visualization, envision a mirror within this landscape. You can approach the mirror to peer into your inner world.

4. Reflection Questions:
   - What do you see as you gaze into the mirror? Take note of your initial thoughts, feelings, or any images that come to mind.
   - Reflect on your present emotions. Are there underlying emotions you've been neglecting or avoiding? Allow yourself to acknowledge and explore these feelings with gentleness and curiosity.
   Please consider your expectations, fears, or desires regarding this journey of self-discovery. Are there any aspects you feel hesitant or eager to explore? Please make sure to note this without judgment.

5. Journaling Practice:
   - Open your journal or a blank piece of paper. Write down your reflections from the visualization exercise. Express your thoughts, emotions, and any insights that emerge.
   - Consider the symbolism of the mirror and what it represents to you in the context of exploring your inner self.

6. Closing Reflection:
   - Take a few moments to reflect on the experience. How do you feel after this initial exploration? Embrace any emotions that arise and acknowledge the courage it takes to embark on this journey.

7. Gratitude Practice:
   - Please be sure to include this opportunity to begin your journey of self-discovery. I appreciate your willingness to explore and embrace your inner landscape.

Remember, this exercise is about initiating the process of self-discovery. Be patient and compassionate with yourself as you embark on this exploration. Feel free to return to this exercise whenever you need to reconnect with your inner self.

Make a list of your best traits

Reflective Question:

What role does self-compassion play in your journey of self-discovery?

"The mind is like an iceberg; it floats with one-seventh of its bulk above water."

Sigmund Freud

Chapter 2

EMBRACING THE CONCEPT OF SHADOWS

In self-exploration, a terrain is often overlooked—the landscape of shadows. Shadows are not merely the absence of light; they are the aspects of ourselves that have been relegated to the periphery of our consciousness. These shadows encompass our unacknowledged emotions, suppressed desires, and hidden fears—the parts of us we may find uncomfortable or challenging to confront.

Embracing the concept of shadows is an integral step in our journey toward self-discovery. Shadows aren't inherent flaws or weaknesses; they are dimensions of our being that hold significant insights and untapped potential. They represent the unexplored territories within, waiting to be illuminated by the light of our awareness.

At times, shadows manifest as unresolved emotions from past experiences. They might surface as insecurities, doubts, or behavior patterns that we find perplexing or unsettling. These aspects often linger in the background, influencing our thoughts, actions, and relationships, even though we might not consciously acknowledge their existence.

To embark on the path of shadow self, it's essential to cultivate a compassionate and nonjudgmental attitude toward ourselves. Instead of viewing these shadows as adversaries, invite them into the light of awareness with an open heart and curiosity. Recognize that they hold keys to self-understanding and growth.

One of the fundamental aspects of shadow work involves introspection—a willingness to explore the origins and implications of these shadowy aspects. To delve deeper into the layers of your consciousness, engage in reflective practices such as journaling, meditation, or creative expression. Through these practices, you can begin to unravel the stories woven within your shadows, understanding their roots and the impact they exert on your life.

Moreover, as you navigate the terrain of shadows, practice self-compassion. Offer yourself kindness and understanding as you encounter these hidden facets of yourself. Embrace vulnerability as a gateway to self-discovery, knowing that acknowledging and integrating these shadows will pave the way for profound healing and personal transformation.

Remember, the shadow self is not about banishing or erasing these aspects of yourself. It's about acknowledging their presence, integrating them into the tapestry of your being, and ultimately, reclaiming your wholeness.

By embracing your shadows, you embark on a courageous journey toward authenticity, self-acceptance, and profound inner illumination.

EXERCISE 2:

EXPLORING TRIGGERED EMOTIONS

Objective: This exercise aims to identify and explore triggered emotions as a gateway to understanding your shadow aspects.

Instructions:

1. Identifying Triggers:
Begin by identifying an emotional trigger that you've recently experienced. Reflect on a situation or interaction that evoked a strong emotional response. It could be an instance of anger, frustration, sadness, or intense emotion.

2. Self-Reflection on Triggers:
   - Take a moment to sit in a comfortable and quiet space. Close your eyes and revisit the triggering situation in your mind. Recreate the scenario in as much detail as possible.
   - Reflect on the emotions that arose during this situation. What was the primary emotion you felt? Were there underlying or secondary emotions linked to the primary feeling?

3. Understanding Triggers:
   - Could you explain why this particular situation triggered such a strong emotional response within you? Reflect on past experiences, beliefs, or unmet needs that might have contributed to this reaction.
   - Explore whether this emotional response aligns with patterns or recurring reactions you've observed in similar situations.

4. Journaling Your Exploration:
   - Open your journal or a blank document. Write down the triggering situation and the emotions you experienced. Reflect on the possible reasons behind this intense emotional reaction.
   - Dive deeper into your feelings. Ask yourself what this trigger reveals about your hidden beliefs, fears, or aspects of yourself that you may have suppressed or ignored.

5. Shadow Integration Reflection:
   - Consider how this triggered emotion might be connected to your shadow aspects. Are there parts of yourself you tend to disown or deny that could relate to this emotion?
   - Reflect on how acknowledging and embracing these shadow aspects could offer insights into your emotional reactions and promote self-understanding.

6. Compassionate Self-Reflection:
   - Practice self-compassion as you explore these triggered emotions. Avoid self-judgment or criticism. Instead, offer kindness and understanding as you delve into these potentially sensitive areas.

7. Closure and Self-Care:
   Conclude the exercise by taking a few deep breaths. Express gratitude for this opportunity to explore your triggered emotions and for the insights you gained.
   - Engage in a self-care activity that comforts you, ensuring you nurture yourself after this reflective exercise.

Remember, this exercise is a step toward understanding the deeper layers of your emotional responses. Approach it with openness and gentleness, allowing yourself to explore the shadow aspects that surface through triggered emotions.

Write down your triggers

Reflective Question:

Describe a moment when you felt the deepest
connection with yourself.

"The goal of individuation is to become an individual, a single, homogeneous being."

Erich Neumann

Chapter 3

TOOLS FOR INNER JOURNEYING

Embarking on the journey of self-discovery and exploring the depths of our inner world requires tools and practices that guide beacons along the path. These tools act as companions, aiding us in navigating the complexities of our inner landscape and fostering a deeper connection with our authentic selves.

In this chapter, we'll explore a variety of tools and techniques designed to facilitate your inner journey. Remember, these tools are not rigid prescriptions but invitations to discover what resonates most with your self-exploration journey.

1. Mindfulness and Meditation: Cultivating mindfulness and engaging in meditation are fundamental tools for inner journeying. Mindfulness allows us to observe our thoughts, emotions, and sensations with nonjudgmental awareness. Through focused breathing, guided visualization, or mantra repetition, meditation creates space for introspection and inner peace.

2. Journaling: Journaling can be an invaluable tool for self-reflection. Writing down your thoughts, emotions, dreams, and experiences provides a tangible record of your inner landscape. Journaling serves as a mirror reflecting the nuances of your inner world, offering clarity and insight into your thoughts and feelings.

3. Creative Expression: Engaging in creative endeavors—painting, music, dance, writing, or any form of artistic expression—can be a powerful means of delving into your subconscious mind. Through creativity, you can access deeper layers of emotions and insights, allowing your inner world to unfold in expressive and transformative ways.

4. Therapeutic Practices: Exploring therapeutic modalities such as psychotherapy, counseling, or group therapy sessions can provide structured support for your inner journey. These practices offer a safe space to explore your inner world with the guidance of trained professionals, facilitating healing and self-discovery.

5. Nature Connection: Connecting with nature can be a profound tool for inner exploration. Spending time outdoors, practicing mindfulness in natural settings, or simply immersing yourself in the beauty of the natural world can foster a sense of tranquility and connectedness, encouraging introspection and inner harmony.

6. Self-Compassion and Gratitude:
Cultivating self-compassion and gratitude serve as essential tools on the journey within. Practicing self-compassion allows us to embrace our vulnerabilities with kindness. At the same time, gratitude helps us appreciate the richness of our experiences, fostering a positive outlook on our inner and outer worlds.

As you engage with these tools, remember that the essence of inner journeying lies not only in the tools themselves but in the intention and commitment you bring to your explorations. Each tool offers a gateway to deeper self-awareness, guiding you toward embracing the vastness of your inner depths.

EXERCISE 3:

UNCOVERING UNCONSCIOUS BELIEFS

Objective: This exercise aims to uncover and examine unconscious beliefs that may influence your perceptions, behaviors, and emotions.

Instructions:

1. Relaxed Setting Preparation:
Find a quiet and comfortable space to relax and focus without interruptions. Sit comfortably and take a few deep breaths to center yourself.

2. Identification of Recurring Patterns:
   - Reflect on recurring patterns—consistent themes in your thoughts, behaviors, or relationships. Identify any repetitive thoughts, reactions, or situations that stand out.

3. Journaling for Self-Reflection:
   - Open your journal or a blank document. Write down these recurring patterns or beliefs that you've identified. Describe how these patterns manifest in your life and how they make you feel.

4. Questioning the Beliefs:
   - Select one of the recurring patterns or beliefs you've listed. You can challenge it by asking yourself probing questions. For instance:
      - What might be the origin of this belief?
      - How does this belief affect my perception of myself and others?
      - Does this belief align with my current values and goals?
      - Have I inherited or internalized this belief from external sources?
      - What evidence supports or contradicts this belief?

5. Exploring Contradicting Evidence:
   - Explore any evidence or experiences that contradict the identified belief. Consider moments in your life where the belief didn't hold or instances where you acted against this belief.

6. Reframing the Belief:
   - Experiment with reframing the belief in a more empowering or affirming manner. You can transform it into a belief that aligns better with your authentic self or current aspirations.

7. Visual Representation:
   - Create a visual representation of this belief system. Could you draw a diagram or mind map showing how this belief is interconnected with your thoughts, emotions, and actions?

8. Closing Reflection and Affirmation:
   - Please put the exercise in by reflecting on your insights. Write down an affirmation or a statement that counters the old belief and aligns with the reframed belief you've created.

9. Gratitude and Self-Care:
   - Express gratitude for this self-exploration journey. Engage in a self-care activity that rejuvenates and uplifts your spirits.

Remember, this exercise is about uncovering unconscious beliefs with curiosity and openness. Approach this self-reflection process without judgment, allowing yourself to challenge and transform beliefs that no longer serve your growth.

Identify Your Recurring Patterns

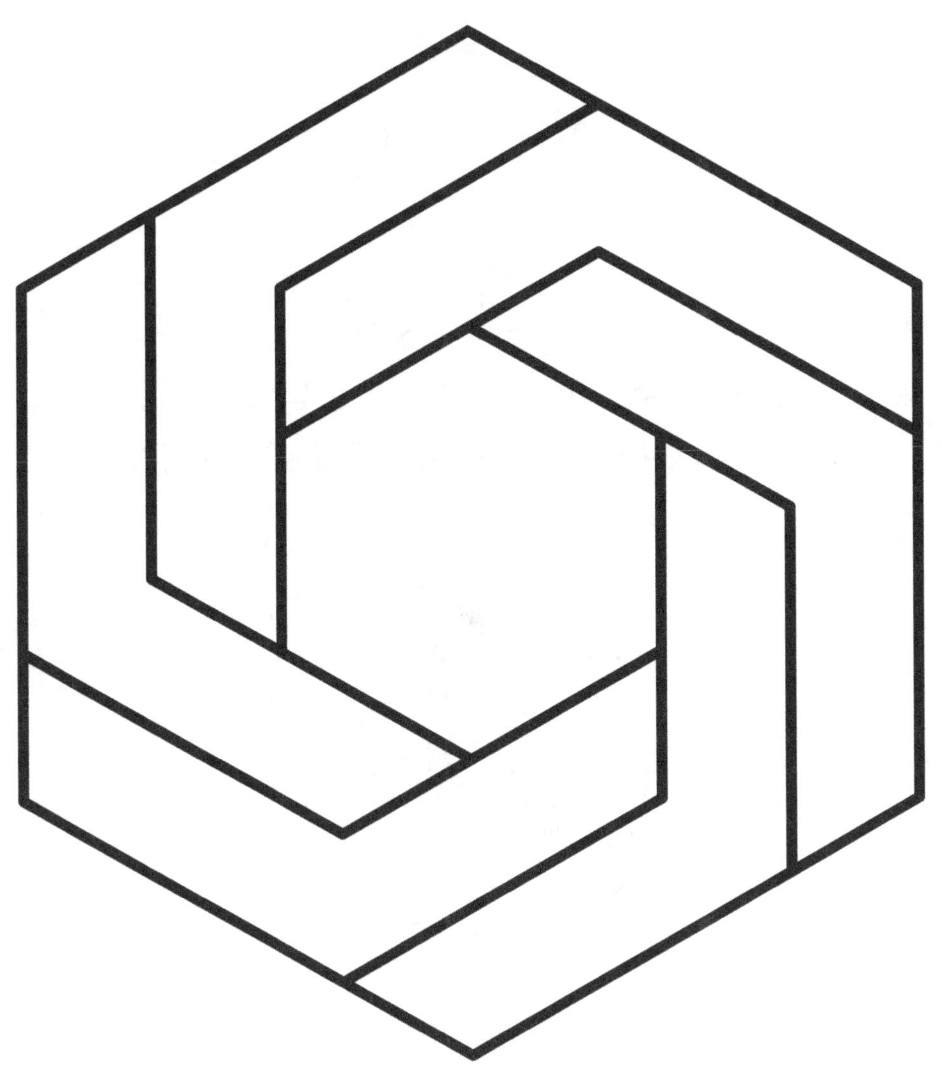

Reflective Question:

Reflect on a past challenge. How did it
contribute to your personal growth?

Part II:

EMBRACING THE SHADOWS

"Dreams are the guiding words of the soul. Why should I henceforth not love my dreams and not make their riddling images into objects of my daily consideration?"

Marie-Louise von Franz

Chapter 4

IDENTIFYING AND ACKNOWLEDGING SHADOWS

Within the vast expanse of our inner landscape, shadows dwell—an enigmatic realm harboring aspects of ourselves that often remain obscured or ignored. Identifying and acknowledging these shadows is crucial in our journey toward self-discovery and inner healing.

Shadows manifest in various forms—unprocessed emotions, unresolved past experiences, suppressed desires, and unrecognized aspects of our personalities. Though hidden from conscious view, these shadows profoundly influence our thoughts, behaviors, and relationships.

Identifying shadows requires a gentle yet deliberate examination of our inner world. It calls for a willingness to turn our gaze inward and courageously confront the aspects of ourselves that may evoke discomfort or unease. To embark on this journey of recognition, consider the following steps:

1. Self-Observation: Cultivate a practice of self-observation. Pay attention to recurring patterns in your thoughts, reactions, and emotional responses. Notice moments of inner conflict, resistance, or discomfort, as they often serve as signposts pointing toward underlying shadows.

2. Exploring Triggers: Shadows often reveal themselves through triggers—events, situations, or interactions that evoke intense emotional reactions. Explore these triggers with curiosity and inquire into the underlying reasons for such responses, unraveling the layers of emotions they uncover.

3. Unearthing Unconscious Beliefs: Engage in introspective practices, such as journaling or dialogue with trusted individuals, to uncover unconscious beliefs that shape your perceptions and behaviors. These beliefs, often rooted in past experiences or societal conditioning, might contribute to forming shadows.

4. Facing Unacknowledged Emotions: Allow yourself to sit with and acknowledge emotions that have been buried or suppressed. These emotions—such as fear, anger, shame, or grief—might reside within the shadows, waiting to be recognized and embraced with compassion.

5. Seeking Clarity and Perspective: Engage in practices that offer clarity and perspective, such as meditation, mindfulness, or seeking guidance from mentors or therapists. These practices facilitate a deeper understanding of the shadows, allowing you to navigate them more easily.

Remember, identifying and acknowledging shadows requires patience, self-compassion, and an attitude of nonjudgment. It is not about assigning blame or criticizing oneself but about shining the light of awareness on the hidden corners of our being.

Acknowledging these shadows, we take the initial steps toward reclaiming our inner wholeness. Embracing these aspects with acceptance and understanding paves the way for profound self-discovery and healing, fostering a deeper connection with our authentic selves.

EXERCISE 4:

EMOTIONAL LANDSCAPE JOURNALING

Objective: This exercise aims to deepen self-awareness by exploring and processing emotions through journaling.

Instructions:

1. Preparation for Journaling:
   - Set aside dedicated time for this exercise in a quiet, comfortable space. Please keep your journal or a blank notebook and a pen ready.

2. Mindfulness and Emotional Awareness:
   - Take a few deep breaths to center yourself. Close your eyes and scan your body, noticing any present emotions or sensations. Acknowledge and name these emotions without judgment.

3. Emotion Identification:
   - Open your journal and list various emotions (e.g., joy, sadness, anger, fear, gratitude, contentment). Could you leave space beside each emotion for writing?

4. Reflective Journaling:
   – Select one emotion from your list that stands out most now. Could you write down the chosen emotion at the top of a new page?
   – Reflect on the prompts related to the chosen emotion:
     – What triggers or situations usually evoke this emotion in me?
     – How does this emotion manifest in my body? Are there physical sensations associated with it?
     – Can I recall past experiences linked to this emotion? How did I handle them?
     – What thoughts or beliefs often accompany this emotion?
     – How does this emotion influence my actions and interactions with others?
     – Is there anything I can learn or understand from experiencing this emotion?

5. Free-Flow Expression:
   – Allow yourself to write about the chosen emotion freely. Please write without censoring or judging your thoughts. Let your emotions guide the words onto the paper.

6. Reflection and Integration:
   – After journaling, take a moment to reflect on what you've written. Look at any patterns, insights, or revelations from this exploration.

7. Gratitude and Self-Care:
   – I am grateful for your willingness to explore your emotional landscape. After this reflective journaling session, engage in a self-care practice that brings comfort and relaxation.

8. Repeat and Explore Other Emotions:
   - In subsequent journaling sessions, explore other emotions from your list using a similar reflective approach. Dedicate separate pages to each emotion to delve deeper into your emotional landscape.

Remember, this exercise is about cultivating emotional awareness and self-understanding through journaling. Approach it with openness and a willingness to explore your inner emotional world without judgment.

Reflective Question:

What are three values you hold dearly, and
how do they shape your decisions?

"The question for me always is how to move from the soul as starting point to the soul as perspective."

James Hillman

Chapter 5

SHADOW WORK TECHNIQUES AND PRACTICES

Engaging in shadow work techniques and practices becomes essential as we continue our self-discovery and inner exploration journey. Shadow work involves actively addressing, integrating, and transforming the aspects of ourselves that reside in the shadows of our consciousness. This chapter delves into various techniques to facilitate this transformative process:

1. Journaling for Shadow Exploration: Utilize your journal as a sacred space for shadow work. Dedicate time to write about recurring patterns, intense emotions, and moments of inner conflict. Engage in free-flow writing or structured prompts to delve deeper into the shadows that surface.

2. Dialogue and Inner Exploration: Engage in internal dialogues or imaginary conversations with different aspects of yourself. This technique allows for a deeper understanding of conflicting emotions or beliefs, fostering integration and self-awareness.

3. Visualization and Inner Child Work: Use visualization techniques to connect with your inner child—the younger versions of yourself that hold unprocessed emotions and experiences. Nurturing and healing your inner child provides profound emotional healing and growth.

4. Emotional Release and Expression: Explore methods of emotional release and expression, such as artistic endeavors, movement, or vocal expression. Allow yourself to express emotions held within the shadows, facilitating catharsis and transformation.

5. Shadow Integration through Meditation: Practice meditation focused on acknowledging and integrating shadow aspects. Through mindfulness and self-compassion, invite these shadows into your awareness, allowing them to be seen and accepted without judgment.

6. Dreamwork and Symbolism: Pay attention to your dreams, often gateways to the unconscious mind. Analyze dream symbols and themes, seeking insights into unresolved emotions or aspects of the self waiting to be acknowledged.

7. Therapeutic Support and Guidance: Consider seeking guidance from therapists, counselors, or shadow work facilitators. Professional support provides a structured and safe environment for exploring more profound aspects of yourself and facilitating transformation.

It's essential to approach shadow work with patience, self-compassion, and a willingness to embrace discomfort. These practices are not quick fixes but pathways to inner transformation and integration. Each technique offers a unique entry point into the shadows, guiding you toward greater self-awareness and wholeness.

By engaging in shadow work techniques and practices, you embark on a journey of profound inner alchemy—transmuting shadows into sources of wisdom, healing, and empowerment. Embrace this transformative process as an essential part of your journey toward self-discovery and holistic growth.

EXERCISE 5:

MINDFUL SELF-COMPASSION MEDITATION

Objective: This exercise aims to cultivate self-compassion through a guided mindfulness meditation.

Instructions:

1. Preparation
  - Find a quiet and comfortable space where you won't be disturbed. Sit or lie relaxed, ensuring you feel comfortable and supported.
  - Set a manageable timer for your meditation practice, such as 10 to 15 minutes.

2. Grounding and Centering:
  - Close your eyes gently. Begin by taking a few deep breaths. Inhale slowly through your nose, allowing your abdomen to rise, and exhale gently through your mouth, releasing any tension.

3. Body Scan:
   - Start by bringing awareness to different body parts, beginning from your toes and slowly moving upward. Notice any sensations, tension, or areas of ease in each body part without trying to change anything.

4. Focus on Breathing:
   - Shift your attention to your breath. Notice the natural rhythm of your breath—its rise and fall. Focus on the sensation of breathing in and out, using your breath as an anchor to the present moment.

5. Self-Compassion Affirmations:
   - Begin to repeat self-compassionate affirmations silently or aloud. You can use phrases like:
      - "May I be kind to myself in moments of difficulty."
      - "May I embrace myself with love and acceptance."
      - "May I find peace and ease in moments of pain or suffering."

6. Open-hearted Compassion:
   - Visualize someone you care about deeply—a loved one or a mentor. Imagine sending them feelings of compassion, love, and kindness. Hold onto these feelings as you continue the meditation.

7. Extending Compassion to Yourself:
   - Now, turn this compassionate energy towards yourself. Picture yourself in your mind's eye. Offer the same feelings of compassion, love, and kindness that you extended to the person you care about.

8. Closing the Practice:
  - As the meditation time ends, take a few moments to bring your awareness back to your surroundings. Slowly open your eyes and gently stretch to conclude the practice.

9. Reflection and Journaling:
  - After the meditation, take some time to reflect on your experience. Journal about any emotions, sensations, or thoughts that arose during the practice. Note any insights or changes in how you feel.

10. Gratitude and Self-Care:
  - Express gratitude to yourself for dedicating this time to self-compassion. Engage in a self-care activity that resonates with you, nurturing your mind and body after the meditation.

Make a List of Your Feelings

Reflective Question:

How do you handle moments of uncertainty or
change in your life?

"The doors to the world of the wild Self are few but precious. If you have a deep scar, that is a door, if you have an old, old story, that is a door. If you love the sky and the water so much you almost cannot bear it, that is a door."

Clarissa Pinkola Estes

Chapter 6

OVERCOMING RESISTANCE TO INNER GROWTH

Embarking on the path of self-discovery and shadow work often encounters resistance—a natural response from fear, uncertainty, or ingrained habits. This chapter explores strategies to overcome resistance and embrace the transformative potential of your inner journey:

1. Acknowledging Resistance: Begin by acknowledging the presence of resistance. Recognize that resistance is a natural response to stepping out of comfort zones and exploring uncharted territories. By acknowledging its existence, you create space for understanding and addressing it.

2. Cultivating Self-Compassion: Practice self-compassion when facing resistance. Treat yourself with kindness and understanding. Acknowledge that resistance is not a sign of weakness but a signal that you are venturing into meaningful and transformative territory.

3. Identifying Underlying Fears: Dive deeper into the underlying fears or beliefs contributing to resistance. Are past experiences, societal expectations, or self-imposed limitations influencing your reluctance to delve into the shadows? Please take care of these underlying factors carefully.

4. Shifting Perspectives: Challenge limiting beliefs by reframing perspectives. View resistance as a sign of growth rather than an obstacle. Embrace discomfort as a catalyst for learning and expansion, recognizing that transformation often emerges from moments of pain.

5. Taking Incremental Steps: Break down your inner journey into manageable steps. Rather than overwhelming yourself with the enormity of the process, focus on small, achievable actions. Celebrate each step forward, no matter how small, as a victory in your journey.

6. Creating Supportive Environments: Surround yourself with supportive communities, mentors, or individuals who understand and encourage your inner journey. Seek inspiration from others who have navigated similar paths and learn from their experiences.

7. Practicing Mindfulness and Patience: Cultivate mindfulness to observe resistance without judgment. Practice patience and gentleness with yourself as you navigate through challenging emotions and moments of resistance. Remember that inner growth is a continuous process that unfolds at its own pace.

8. Revisiting Intentions and Motivations: Reconnect with the intentions and motivations behind your inner journey. Could you remind yourself of the reasons that prompted you to embark on this transformative path, reigniting your sense of purpose and commitment?

Overcoming resistance is an integral part of the transformative journey toward self-discovery. Embrace these strategies as tools to navigate through resistance, allowing you to step into the fullness of your authentic self and embrace the profound growth awaiting you within the shadows.

EXERCISE 6:

CLARIFYING YOUR CORE VALUES

Objective: This exercise aims to help you identify and prioritize your core values and guiding principles that define what matters most to you.

Instructions:

1. Quiet Reflection Time:
   - Find a quiet and comfortable space where you can reflect without distractions. Have your journal or a blank sheet of paper and a pen ready.

2. Defining Values:
   - Start by considering various aspects of life, such as relationships, career, and personal growth. I'd like you to reflect on moments when you felt most fulfilled, proud, or aligned with your authentic self. What values were present in those moments?

3. Identify Potential Values:
  - Create a list of potential values that resonate with you.
Examples include authenticity, compassion, creativity, family,
growth, integrity, justice, kindness, resilience. Could you
write down as many as come to mind?

4. Ranking Values:
  - Review the list and prioritize your top ten values. Consider
which values resonate with you and are non-negotiable in
defining who you are and how you want to live your life.
Write them in order of priority.

5. Reflective Questions:
   - For each value on your list, ask yourself:
    - What does this value mean to me personally?
    - How does this value show up in my daily life or
decisions?
    - Am I currently living in alignment with this value? If not,
why?
    - How would honoring this value more consciously
enhance my life?

6. Narrowing Down to Core Values:
  - Review your top ten values and identify the three to five
values that feel essential and deeply resonant with your
authentic self. These are your core values.

7. Writing Your Personal Values Statement:
   - Craft a personal values statement summarizing your core
values. This statement could be a sentence or a short
paragraph that encapsulates your most cherished values and
what they mean to you.

8. Reflection and Integration:
   - Reflect on the process of identifying your core values. Consider how these values align with your life choices, goals, and relationships. Journal about any insights or feelings that arose during this exercise.

9. Gratitude and Self-Appreciation:
   - Please be sure to express gratitude for clarifying your core values. Acknowledge the importance of these values in shaping your life. Engage in an activity that signifies honoring these values.

Reflective Question:

Describe an experience that taught you an important life lesson.

Part III:

NAVIGATING THE DEPTHS

"The privilege of a lifetime is
being who you are."

Joseph Campbell

Chapter 7

HEALING THROUGH SELF-REFLECTION

Self-reflection is a powerful healing catalyst, offering a gateway to understanding, acceptance, and transformation. This chapter delves into the ways self-reflection contributes to the healing process during your journey of self-discovery:

1. Cultivating Awareness Through Reflection: Engage in regular moments of introspection and self-inquiry. Set aside time to reflect on your thoughts, emotions, and experiences without judgment. Cultivate a sense of curiosity about your inner world, allowing insights to emerge.

2. Exploring Patterns and Triggers: Reflect on recurring patterns or triggers. Respond to situations or emotions that elicit strong reactions and delve into their underlying causes. Awareness of these patterns provides opportunities for healing and growth.

3. Embracing Vulnerability: Embrace vulnerability as a gateway to healing. Reflect on moments of vulnerability with compassion rather than avoidance. Understand that vulnerability allows for deeper connections with oneself and others, fostering emotional healing.

4. Self-Forgiveness and Compassion: Reflect on past experiences or self-imposed judgments to forgive and offer yourself compassion. Practice letting go of self-criticism and embrace self-compassion as a healing balm for emotional wounds.

5. Integrating Lessons from Challenges: Reflect on challenges and hardships as opportunities for growth. Explore the lessons from difficult experiences, acknowledging their role in shaping your resilience and wisdom.

6. Gratitude and Positive Reflection: Cultivate a practice of gratitude through reflection. Reflect on moments of joy, accomplishments, or acts of kindness—acknowledge and appreciate them. Gratitude serves as a powerful tool for healing and shifting perspectives.

7. Mindful Self-Compassion Meditation: Engage in mindful self-compassion meditations. These practices combine mindfulness and self-compassion to cultivate a kinder, more accepting relationship with yourself, fostering emotional healing and resilience.

8. Writing for Self-Reflection: Utilize writing as a tool for self-reflection—Journal about your inner experiences, thoughts, and emotions. Writing provides a tangible outlet for processing and understanding your inner world.

Remember, self-reflection is an ongoing practice—a continuous dialogue with yourself that unfolds over time. Embrace self-reflection as an integral part of your healing journey, allowing it to illuminate the path toward self-discovery, emotional wellness, and inner harmony.

EXERCISE 7:

EXPLORING AND ESTABLISHING PERSONAL BOUNDARIES

Objective: This exercise aims to help you identify, understand, and establish healthy personal boundaries in various areas of your life.

Instructions:

1. Reflecting on Personal Boundaries:
  - Find a quiet and comfortable space where you can reflect without distractions. Have your journal or a blank sheet of paper and a pen ready.
  - Reflect on different areas of your life—relationships, work, personal space. Think about instances where you felt uncomfortable, resentful, or stressed. Were your boundaries crossed in those situations?

2. Identifying Boundary Indicators:
 - List situations or behaviors that indicate your boundaries might have been violated. These could be instances where you felt overwhelmed, taken advantage of, or not respected. Note the emotions associated with these situations.

3. Defining Your Boundaries:
 - Write down what specific boundaries mean to you in various areas of life (e.g., physical space, time, emotional well-being, relationships). Define what is acceptable and unacceptable to you in each area.

4. Reflective Questions:
 - For each area of your life, ask yourself:
 - What are my limits or boundaries in this area?
 - How do I feel when my boundaries are respected versus when violated?
 - What actions or behaviors from others make me feel uncomfortable or disrespected?
 - How can I communicate my boundaries effectively to others?

5. Setting Personal Boundaries:
 - Identify three specific boundaries crucial for your well-being and happiness from your reflections. Could you write them down clearly and concisely?

6. Boundary Communication Practice:
 - Practice communicating your boundaries assertively and respectfully. Role-play or write out possible scenarios where you might need to assert these boundaries with someone else.

7. Reflective Integration:
  - Reflect on the process of exploring and setting your boundaries. Consider how asserting these boundaries could positively impact your life. Journal about any insights or emotions that surfaced during this exercise.

8. Gratitude and Self-Acknowledgment:
 - I am grateful for your efforts to understand and establish your boundaries. Acknowledge the importance of respecting your boundaries for your well-being.

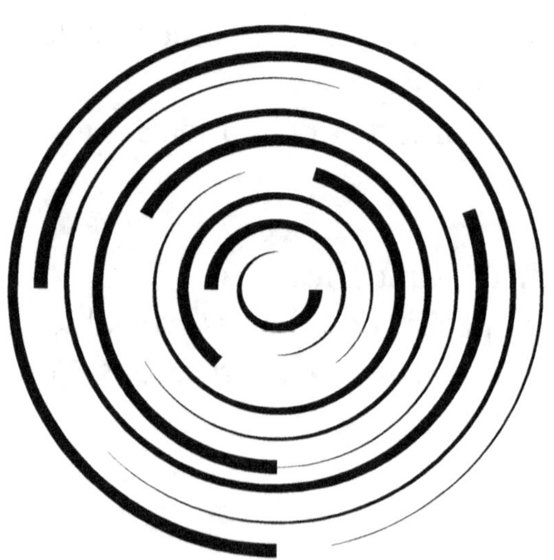

Identify Your Personal Boundaries

Describe a situation where setting boundaries positively impacted your life.

"Out of your vulnerabilities
will come your strength."

Sigmund Freud

Chapter 8

HONORING VULNERABILITY AND AUTHENTICITY

In the landscape of self-discovery and inner exploration, honoring vulnerability and authenticity becomes a pivotal aspect of embracing your depths. This chapter delves into the significance of vulnerability and authenticity on your journey:

1. Understanding Vulnerability: Recognize vulnerability as the gateway to authenticity. Embrace vulnerability as the courage to show up authentically, allowing yourself to be seen, heard, and understood without pretense or masks.

2. Embracing Imperfection: Embrace the imperfections that make you uniquely human. Acknowledge that imperfection is an integral part of the human experience and serves as a wellspring of authenticity.

3. Cultivating Self-Awareness: Engage in self-awareness practices to deepen your understanding of yourself. Reflect on your values, beliefs, and aspirations. This self-awareness fosters an authentic connection with your inner truth.

4. Expressing Authenticity in Relationships: Practice authenticity in your relationships.

Communicate openly, honestly, and vulnerably with others. Cultivate connections that honor your true self, fostering meaningful and genuine relationships.

5. Releasing the Fear of Judgment: Challenge the fear of judgment by embracing your authenticity. Recognizing authenticity invites connection and resonance with those who align with your true self, while others' decisions do not define your worth or authenticity.

6. Living in Alignment with Values: Align your actions with your core values. Living authentically involves making choices that resonate with your beliefs and principles, allowing you to live a life congruent with your authentic self.

7. Practicing Self-Validation: Validate your experiences, emotions, and perspectives without seeking external validation. Trust in your inner wisdom and honor your truths, fostering a more profound sense of self-acceptance.

8. Celebrating Growth and Evolution: Embrace the evolution of your authentic self. Recognize that authenticity is not stagnant; it evolves with self-discovery and growth. Celebrate the continual unfolding of your genuine identity.

Remember, honoring vulnerability and authenticity is not a destination but a continuous practice—an ongoing commitment to embracing your true self. By cultivating vulnerability and authenticity, you pave the way for deeper connections, genuine self-expression, and a more fulfilling journey of self-discovery.

EXERCISE 8:

BUILDING EMOTIONAL RESILIENCE THROUGH AFFIRMATIONS

Objective: This exercise strengthens emotional resilience by cultivating positive affirmations for challenging situations.

Instructions:

1. Preparation:
   - Find a quiet and comfortable space where you can focus without interruptions. Have your journal or a blank sheet of paper and a pen ready.

2. Identifying Challenging Situations:
   - Reflect on past or potential challenging situations you've encountered or may encounter. These could include moments of stress, uncertainty, self-doubt, or adversity.

3. Recognizing Positive Qualities:
   - List positive qualities or strengths you possess that have helped you navigate difficult situations. Consider traits like resilience, adaptability, courage, and compassion.

4. Crafting Resilience Affirmations:
   - Use the positive qualities you listed to create affirmations that reinforce your emotional resilience. For example:
     - "I am resilient and can overcome any challenge that comes my way."

- "I embrace change with courage and adaptability."
- "I am capable of finding opportunities in adversity."

5. Personalizing Affirmations:
   - Please tailor these affirmations to suit specific challenging situations you've identified. Craft affirmations that directly address the concerns or uncertainties you might face.

6. Repetition and Affirmation Practice:
   - Repeat these affirmations aloud or silently several times a day, especially in moments of stress or uncertainty. Practice saying them with conviction and belief in their truth.

7. Visualization Exercise:
   - Close your eyes and visualize yourself facing a challenging situation. Please just repeat your chosen affirmations while you imagine yourself handling the situation with resilience and confidence.

8. Reflection and Integration:
   - Reflect on the experience of using affirmations to build emotional resilience. Keep in mind any shifts in your mindset or feelings of empowerment. Journal about your reflections.

9. Gratitude and Self-Appreciation:
   - Express gratitude to yourself for taking steps to strengthen your emotional resilience. Acknowledge your efforts and commitment to nurturing your resilience.

Make a List of Your Strengths

Describe a moment when you felt a strong
sense of resilience.

"The spiritual journey involves going beyond hope and fear, stepping into unknown territory, continually moving forward."

Murray Stein

Chapter 9

CULTIVATING SELF-COMPASSION

Self-compassion serves as a guiding light on the path of self-discovery and inner healing. This chapter explores the significance of cultivating self-compassion and its transformative impact on your journey:

1. Understanding Self-Compassion: Recognize self-compassion as an act of kindness and understanding toward yourself, especially in times of struggle or difficulty. It involves extending the same compassion you offer others to yourself.

2. Practicing Mindful Awareness: Engage in mindful awareness of your inner dialogue and self-talk. Notice moments of self-criticism or judgment and gently redirect these thoughts toward self-kindness and understanding.

3. Embracing Imperfection with Kindness: Embrace imperfections and shortcomings with kindness. Understand that being imperfect is a part of the human experience and does not diminish your worth.

4. Cultivating a Supportive Inner Voice: Foster a supportive and compassionate inner dialogue. Replace harsh self-talk with words of encouragement and understanding, treating yourself as you would a dear friend.

5. Self-Validation and Acceptance: Practice self-validation and acceptance. Acknowledge and validate your emotions and experiences without judgment. Accept yourself fully, embracing all aspects of your being.

6. Forgiveness and Letting Go: Practice forgiveness toward yourself for past mistakes or perceived shortcomings. Let go of self-blame and guilt, allowing space for healing and growth.

7. Setting Boundaries with Self-Compassion: Establish healthy boundaries with kindness and self-respect. Recognize the importance of self-care and honoring your needs without feeling guilty or selfish.

8. Gratitude and Self-Appreciation: Cultivate gratitude for yourself. Acknowledge your strengths, achievements, and efforts. Celebrate your journey with an appreciation for your resilience and growth.

9. Connecting with Common Humanity: Recognize that suffering, challenges, and imperfections are universal experiences. Embrace a sense of common humanity, understanding that you are not alone in your struggles.

Cultivating self-compassion involves a commitment to treating yourself with the same care, empathy, and understanding you would offer others. By nurturing self-compassion, you create a nurturing and supportive inner environment conducive to self-discovery, healing, and personal growth.

EXERCISE 9:

GRATITUDE JOURNALING FOR SELF-DISCOVERY

Objective: This exercise aims to cultivate gratitude as a means of self-discovery and personal growth.

Instructions:

1. Setting Up Your Gratitude Journal:
   - Allocate a dedicated journal or section in your existing journal for gratitude journaling. Have a pen or pencil ready.

2. Mindful Reflection:
   - Sit in a quiet, comfortable space where you can reflect without disturbance. Take a few deep breaths to center yourself and bring your focus to the present moment.

3. Reflecting on Gratitude:
   - Begin by reflecting on aspects of your life for which you feel grateful. It could be simple things like experiences, relationships, opportunities, or qualities within yourself.

4. Daily Gratitude Entries:
   - Each day, preferably in the morning or before bedtime, write down three to five things you are grateful for. Could you be specific and descriptive? For instance:
     - "I'm grateful for my supportive conversation with a friend today."

- "I appreciate the peaceful moments during my morning walk."
- "I'm thankful for my ability to learn and grow from challenging situations."

5. Exploring Gratitude Themes:
   - Once a week, explore a specific gratitude theme. For example, focus on gratitude for relationships, personal growth, nature, opportunities, or the present moment. Write about why these themes are meaningful to you.

6. Mindful Reflection and Visualization:
   - After writing down your daily gratitudes, take a moment to reflect on each entry. Close your eyes and visualize the moment or experience for which you've expressed gratitude. Feel the emotions associated with it.

7. Self-Reflection Prompts:
   - Occasionally, incorporate self-reflection prompts related to gratitude. For instance:
     - How does practicing gratitude impact my overall mood and mindset?
     - Have there been shifts in my perception or attitude since starting this gratitude practice?
     - How does expressing gratitude affect my relationships and interactions with others?

8. Weekly Review and Gratitude Recap:
   - At the end of each week, review your gratitude entries.

Reflect on the patterns, recurring themes, or newfound aspects you're grateful for. Summarize the week's gratitude highlights.

9. Gratitude Expression Beyond Journaling:
   - Extend your gratitude practice beyond the journal by expressing appreciation to others. Write a note of thanks or express gratitude to someone who positively impacted your life.

10. Gratitude Integration and Self-Care:
   - Reflect on the positive effects of this gratitude practice on your well-being and personal growth. You can engage in self-care activities that complement your feelings of gratitude.

What habits or practices help you maintain mental clarity and focus?

Part IV:

INTEGRATION AND TRANSFORMATION

"In our depths are the recollections of millions of years."

Erich Neumann

Chapter 10

INTEGRATING SHADOW ASPECTS

Integrating shadow aspects marks a significant phase in self-discovery and inner harmony. This chapter explores the process of integrating these hidden facets into our conscious awareness:

1. Awareness and Acceptance: Begin by fostering awareness and acceptance of your shadow aspects. Acknowledge and embrace these facets without judgment or aversion, understanding their inherent value in shaping your experiences.

2. Exploration and Understanding: Engage in deep exploration and understanding of your shadows. Investigate their origins, the beliefs associated with them, and the emotions they evoke. This exploration provides insight into their influence on your life.

3. Confrontation with Compassion: Confront your shadow aspects with compassion and gentleness. Approach them as teachers rather than adversaries, recognizing the lessons and wisdom they offer.

4. Integration through Self-Reflection: Reflect on how your shadows manifest in daily life.

Look at their influence on your thoughts, behaviors, and relationships. This self-reflection facilitates conscious integration.

5. Embracing the Unseen Self: Embrace the unseen aspects of yourself. Integrate them into your self-concept, understanding that they contribute to your wholeness and authenticity.

6. Expressive Integration: Engage in expressive practices to aid integration. Artistic expression, writing, or other creative outlets allow for a tangible representation of your integrated self.

7. Self-Compassion in Integration: Practice self-compassion during the integration process. Understand that it's natural to encounter resistance or discomfort when integrating shadow aspects. Treat yourself with kindness and patience.

8. Reaping the Fruits of Integration: Embrace the transformation that arises from integration. Notice how the integrated aspects contribute to personal growth, resilience, and a deeper understanding of yourself.

9. Continuous Integration Journey: Recognize that integration is an ongoing journey. As you evolve, new aspects of your shadows may surface, requiring continual integration and acceptance.

Integrating shadow aspects is not about eradicating or changing these facets but acknowledging, understanding, and integrating them into the tapestry of your being. You foster a profound sense of self-awareness, inner harmony, and authenticity through integration.

EXERCISE 10:

EXPLORING CREATIVITY THROUGH FREE-WRITING

Objective: This exercise aims to tap into your creative potential through free writing, allowing ideas to flow without constraints or judgment.

Instructions:

1. Preparing for Free Writing:
   - You can find a quiet and comfortable space to concentrate without interruptions. Have your journal or a blank sheet of paper and a pen ready.

2. Mindful Centering:
   - Take a few deep breaths to center yourself and bring your focus to the present moment. Relax your body and clear your mind of any distractions.

3. Setting a Time Limit:
   - Set a timer for 10 to 15 minutes. This exercise involves continuous writing without stopping, so the timer will help maintain focus and flow.

4. Begin Free-Writing:
   - Start writing without worrying about grammar, spelling, or structure. Write whatever comes to mind, allowing thoughts to flow naturally. If you get stuck, write "I'm stuck" and continue writing.

5. Explore Creative Prompts:
   - If necessary, please start with a creative prompt or question to kickstart the process. For example:
      - "The most exciting adventure I can imagine is..."
      - "If I had no limitations, I would create..."
      - "My ideal day filled with creativity looks like..."

6. Keep Writing without Stopping:
   - Don't worry about coherence or logic. Let your thoughts lead the way. If your mind goes blank, describe your environment or write about your feelings.

7. Embracing Unexpected Ideas:
   - Embrace unexpected thoughts or ideas that surface. Allow yourself to explore unconventional or imaginative concepts without self-censorship.

8. Reflection and Review:
   - After the time, could you read through what you've written? Underline or highlight any phrases or ideas that resonate or inspire you. Reflect on any patterns or themes that emerged.

9. Creative Project Development:
   - If specific ideas stand out, consider how you might develop them further. Can they be integrated into a creative project, artwork, story, or expression?

10. Gratitude and Creative Nourishment:
 - Express gratitude for the creative flow and ideas that emerged during the free-writing session. Engage in an activity that fuels your creativity, such as sketching, painting, or listening to inspiring music.

How do you embrace and learn from your
mistakes or failures?

"If you've lost focus, just sit down and be still. Take the idea and rock it to and fro. Keep some of it and throw some away, and it will renew itself. You need do no more."

Clarissa Pinkola Estes

Chapter 11

EMBRACING WHOLENESS AND BALANCE

Embracing wholeness and balance is an essential milestone on the path of self-discovery and inner integration. This chapter explores the significance of cultivating a sense of wholeness and balance within oneself:

1. Understanding Wholeness: Wholeness is not the absence of imperfections but the integration of all aspects of the self—the light and the shadow, the perceived strengths and vulnerabilities. Embrace the totality of your being.

2. Harmonizing Polarities: Recognize and reconcile the polarities within yourself. Balance the masculine and feminine energies and active and receptive qualities, fostering an inner equilibrium.

3. Embracing Duality: Embrace the duality inherent in human existence. Acknowledge the interplay of opposing forces within, such as joy and sorrow, certainty and doubt, and find harmony in their coexistence.

4. Alignment with Core Values: Align your actions and choices with your core values. Living in alignment with your values fosters a sense of integrity and congruence, contributing to a feeling of wholeness.

5. Mind-Body Connection: Cultivate a harmonious mind-body connection. Practice mindfulness, meditation, or somatic exercises that allow you to tune into your body's wisdom, fostering a holistic sense of well-being.

6. Integration of Experiences: Consider your life experiences —both pleasant and challenging—integral parts of your journey. Recognize their role in shaping your identity and wisdom.

7. Self-Care and Nurturing: Prioritize self-care and nurturing practices. Attend to your physical, emotional, and mental well-being with kindness and compassion, recognizing their interconnectedness.

8. Embracing Change and Adaptability: Embrace change as a constant in life. Cultivate adaptability and resilience, understanding that growth often emerges from moments of transformation and adaptation.

9. Gratitude for Wholeness: Cultivate gratitude for your inherent wholeness. Acknowledge and appreciate the completeness within yourself, fostering a sense of appreciation for the journey you've traversed.

Embracing wholeness and balance involves self-awareness, acceptance, and alignment with one's authentic self. Nurturing this sense of wholeness creates a foundation for inner harmony, resilience, and a fulfilling life journey.

EXERCISE 11:

MINDFUL NATURE WALK

Objective: This exercise aims to deepen mindfulness by immersing oneself in nature and experiencing the present moment with heightened awareness.

Instructions:

1. Choosing a Natural Setting:
   - Find a nearby park, garden, forest trail, beach, or any natural environment that allows you to connect with nature. Could you ensure it's a place where you feel comfortable and safe?

2. Preparing for the WalWalk - Dress comfortably for the weather. Leave electronic devices behind or set them to silent mode to minimize distractions. Bring along a journal or notepad and a pen.

3. Mindful Preparation:
   - Take a moment before walking to stand still and become aware of your surroundings. Take a few deep breaths to ground yourself in the present moment.

4. Setting Intentions:
   - Set an intention for the walk, such as being present, observing nature's details, or finding tranquility. Could you allow this intention to guide your experience?

5. Mindful Observation:
   - Start walking at a comfortable pace, paying attention to each step. Engage your senses by noticing the sights, sounds, smells, and textures around you.
   - Pause frequently to observe nature's details. Notice the colors of leaves, the textures of tree bark, the sounds of birds or rustling leaves, and any scents in the air.

6. Deep Breathing and Connection:
   - Pause intermittently to take deep, mindful breaths. Feel the air entering your lungs and notice how it connects you to the natural environment.

7. Mindful Reflection and Journaling:
   - Take breaks to sit quietly on a bench or find a peaceful spot. Reflect on the sensations and emotions evoked by nature. Write down your thoughts, observations, and feelings in your journal.

8. Gratitude Practice:
   - Practice gratitude for the nature around you. Acknowledge the beauty and serenity it provides. Consider what you're thankful for in this natural setting.

9. Closing Mindfulness Practice:
   - As you finish your walk, take a moment to express gratitude for the experience. Stop, take a few final deep breaths, and appreciate the peace and mindfulness nature has offered you.

10. Reflecting on Insights:
   - After the walk, review your journal notes. I'd like you to reflect on any insights gained, emotions experienced, or newfound connections with nature.

Reflective Question:

Reflect on your relationships. How do they influence your personal growth?

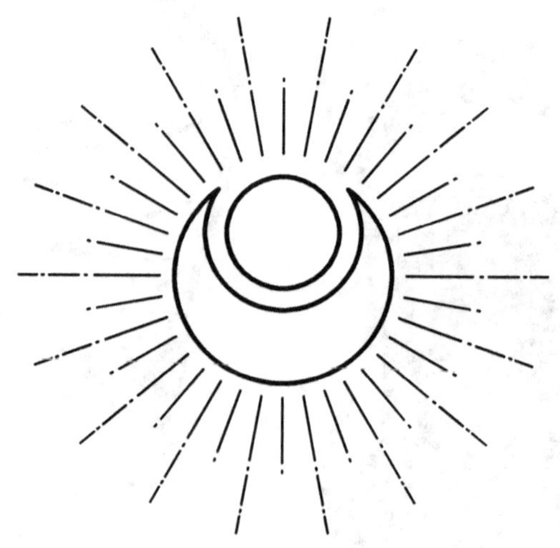

"The unconscious wants truth.
It ceases to speak to those
who want something else more
than truth."

Marie-Louise von Franz

Chapter 12

SUSTAINING GROWTH AND REFLECTION

As your journey of self-discovery continues, sustaining personal growth and engaging in reflective practices becomes paramount. This chapter explores strategies to maintain growth and the importance of ongoing reflection:

1. Cultivating a Growth Mindset: Embrace a growth mindset that perceives challenges as opportunities for learning and growth. Continuously seek new experiences and knowledge to foster personal development.

2. Setting Intentions for Growth: Set clear intentions for personal growth. Define goals aligned with your values and aspirations, allowing continuous evolution and progress.

3. Consistent Self-Reflection: Engage in regular self-reflection. I'd like you to please dedicate time to assess your growth, experiences, and challenges encountered along the journey, fostering a deeper understanding of your evolving self.

4. Adapting to Change and Feedback: Embrace change and feedback as catalysts for growth. Be open to evolving perspectives and adapt to new insights from experiences and feedback.

5. Learning from Adversity: Extract lessons from adversity. View challenges as opportunities for resilience-building and personal transformation, recognizing the strength gained from navigating difficult situations.

6. Celebrating Milestones and Achievements: Celebrate your milestones and achievements. Acknowledge and appreciate the progress made on your journey, reinforcing a positive outlook and motivation for further growth.

7. Engaging in Continued Education and Development: Invest in ongoing education and personal development. Explore new interests, acquire new skills, or engage in activities that nurture your intellectual and emotional growth.

8. Practicing Gratitude and Mindfulness: Cultivate gratitude and mindfulness as daily practices. Appreciate the present moment and express gratitude for the lessons, experiences, and connections contributing to your growth.

9. Sharing and Contributing to Others' Growth: Share insights and support others on their journeys. Contributing to others' growth fosters a sense of fulfillment and reinforces your commitment to continuous learning and development.

10. Honoring Self-Care and Balance: Prioritize self-care and maintain a healthy balance in life. Nurturing your physical, emotional, and mental well-being is essential for sustained growth and resilience.

Sustaining personal growth is an ongoing commitment that requires dedication, self-awareness, and a willingness to embrace the journey with an open heart and mind. Continual reflection and intentional practices pave the way for an enriched and purposeful life journey.

EXERCISE 12:

VISION BOARD CREATION FOR PERSONAL GROWTH

Objective: This exercise aims to visualize and manifest personal growth, aspirations, and goals through a vision board.

Instructions:

1. Gathering Materials:
   - Collect materials for your vision board. You'll need a poster board, corkboard, canvas, magazines, newspapers, printed images, scissors, glue, markers, and other decorative materials.

2. Setting the Intention:
   - Find a quiet, comfortable space to work on your vision board without distractions. Set an intention for this creative process—visualizing your desired personal growth and aspirations.

3. Reflection and Goal Setting:
   - Reflect on the areas of personal growth you wish to focus on—such as career, relationships, health, creativity, and spirituality. Identify specific goals or intentions within these areas.

4. Gathering Visual Inspirations:
   - Browse magazines, online images, or any visuals that resonate with your goals and aspirations. Cut out images, words, or phrases that symbolize or represent your desired personal growth.

5. Arranging and Creating the Vision Board:
   - Start arranging the cut-out images, phrases, or words on your board. Organize them in a way that feels intuitive and inspiring to you. Be creative and allow your intuition to guide the placement.

6. Personalization and Creativity:
   - Add personal touches to your vision board. You can include handwritten affirmations, drawings, or quotes that deeply resonate with your goals and vision for personal growth.

7. Visualizing Your Growth:
   - Once your vision board is complete, take a moment to sit with it. Visualize yourself achieving these goals and experiencing the personal growth depicted on the board. Feel the emotions associated with your envisioned success.

8. Placement and Display:
   - Place your vision board in a prominent location where you'll see it daily—such as your bedroom, office, or a dedicated space at home. Ensure it's visible and serves as a daily reminder of your aspirations.

9. Daily Affirmations and Visualization:
   - Spend a few moments each day looking at your vision board. Engage in positive affirmations and visualize yourself embodying the growth and achievements depicted on the board.

10. Reflection and Action:
   - Reflect on the emotions and motivation your vision board evokes. Take action steps you can take toward reaching the goals represented on the board.

Describe a personal mantra or affirmation that inspires and motivates you.

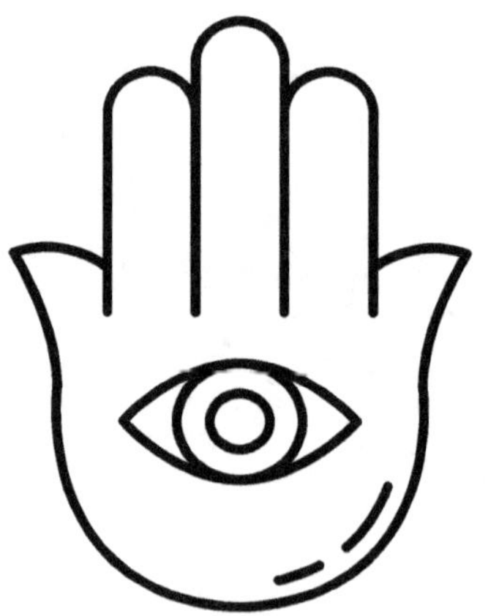

CONCLUSION

EMBRACING THE INFINITE DEPTHS WITHIN

As we conclude this journey of self-discovery together, it's essential to acknowledge that exploring our inner depths is an ever-unfolding odyssey—an infinite voyage rich with complexities, nuances, and profound revelations.

Throughout this expedition, you've delved into the intricate labyrinth of your psyche, courageously exploring the light and shadows that compose the tapestry of your being. You've navigated through the terrain of self-reflection, embraced vulnerability, and dared to confront the hidden facets of your identity.

The journey of self-discovery is not a linear path with a definitive destination but a continuous spiral. This cyclical movement leads us deeper into the essence of our authenticity. It's about honoring the process rather than rushing toward a final destination, understanding that each step, each moment of self-reflection, contributes to our growth and evolution.

As we reflect on the lessons learned and the wisdom gained from traversing our inner landscapes, let us carry forth these guiding principles:

1. Authenticity as a Compass: Let authenticity be your guiding star. Embrace your uniqueness, integrating the light and shadows into the mosaic of your true self.

2. Compassion as a Companion: Cultivate self-compassion as you journey through life. Treat yourself with the same kindness and understanding you extend to others, fostering a nurturing environment for growth.

3. Courage in Vulnerability: Embrace vulnerability as a source of strength. We connect deeply with ourselves and others through vulnerability, forging meaningful bonds.

4. Resilience in Transformation: Embrace change as a catalyst for transformation. Embody resilience in the face of challenges, understanding that growth often arises from moments of discomfort and adaptation.

5. Gratitude for the Journey: Cultivate gratitude for the journey itself. Each experience, whether joyful or challenging, contributes to the richness of your life's narrative.

As we bid adieu to this chapter of our shared exploration, remember that your journey of self-discovery is unique and ongoing. Embrace the infinite depths within you with curiosity, resilience, and boundless self-compassion.

May you continue to navigate the intricacies of your inner world with an open heart and an unwavering commitment to embrace the beauty and complexity of your depths.

Your journey toward self-discovery is a testament to your courage, resilience, and dedication to living an authentic, fulfilling life.

In the grand tapestry of existence, may you always find solace and wisdom in the profound depths of your being.

With deepest regards on your continued journey,

"Life is a process of becoming, a combination of states we have to go through. Where people fail is when they wish to elect a state and remain in it. This is a kind of death."

Murray Stein

www.ingramcontent.com/pod-product-compliance
Lightning Source LLC
Chambersburg PA
CBHW071451130726
47997CB00006B/2323